THE WO

G000021264

THE RIVER GODS
AND DUBLIN'S CUSTOM HOUSE

ELIZABETH HEALY

WOLFHOUND PRESS
& in the US and Canada
The Irish American Book Company

First published in 1998 by
Wolfhound Press Ltd
68 Mountjoy Square
Dublin 1, Ireland
Tel: (353-1) 874 0354
Fax: (353-1) 872 0207

Published in the US and Canada by
The Irish American Book Company
6309 Monarch Park Place
Niwot, Colorado 80503
USA
Tel: (303) 652-2710
Fax: (303) 652-2689

Wolfhound Press receives financial assistance from the Arts Council/An Comhairle
Ealaíon, Dublin.

British Library Cataloguing in Publication Data
A catalogue record for this book is available from the British Library.

ISBN 0-86327-642-3

10 9 8 7 6 5 4 3 2 1

Editorial Consultant: Roberta Reeners
Design and Origination: Design Image
Cover Illustration: Nicola Emoe
Cover Design: Slick Fish Design, Dublin
Printed in the Republic of Ireland by Colour Books, Dublin

For permission to reproduce photographs and other illustrative material, the
publishers are grateful to Dúchas The Heritage Service, David Davison Associates,
Bord Fáilte/The Irish Tourist Board and The National Library of Ireland.

CONTENTS

DUBLIN'S CUSTOM HOUSE

. . . the keystones representing the principal rivers of Ireland, some of which are equal to Michael Angelo . . . are executed by Mr. E. Smith, a native of Ireland.

The keystones worthy of comparison to 'Michael Angelo' are the huge stone heads which decorate the ground-floor arches of Dublin's Custom House. They are allegorical representations of the thirteen principal rivers of Ireland, with the Atlantic Ocean thrown in for good measure. They have come to be known as the River Gods.

Dublin's Custom House is counted among the distinguished buildings of Europe. When it was built during the 1780s, it stood on clear space well down-river from the bustle of the city as it was then. Today, it is partly obscured by the Loop Line Railway Bridge, and the heavy traffic hurtling by in all directions makes it difficult to walk around it at leisure using the semi-circular Beresford Place/Memorial Road, which was more or less designed for the purpose. So the nobility of the Custom House is best appreciated from across the river. But for a good view of the River Gods, it is necessary to approach more closely. Even then, a pair of binoculars is helpful, as the keystones are quite high above the ground.

✳ Dublin's Custom House, viewed from across the River Liffey

James Gandon was the architect. Although an Englishman, most of his great work was done in Ireland, beginning with the Custom House. He was still in his thirties when the question of the commission was first raised. While well regarded in the profession, Gandon had no major work behind him. Furthermore, his knowledge of Ireland was mainly limited to socialising in London with his friend Paul Sandby's Irish cronies. So how did this relatively unknown young man come to be chosen for such a major enterprise – especially at a time when several architects of international standing were, or had already been, at work in Ireland, among them Thomas Ivory, Thomas Cooley and William Chambers? The main reason was that the potential architect had to be approached (and the project got under way) in the strictest secrecy, away from the well-oiled Dublin gossip machine.

The story of the building of the Custom House has many of the elements of an old-fashioned cloak-and-dagger novel, full of intrigue and political skulduggery. During the eighteenth century, Dublin was a brilliant and cosmopolitan city, a place of wealth and fashion. It was a time of rapid expansion, with fine new squares and avenues springing up, reaching away from the old-established centre around Dublin Castle. It was felt that a new bridge was needed farther down-river to service this expansion and connect the wealthy new suburbs.

* James Gandon, architect of the Custom House

But the old Custom House, dating from 1707, stood on Wellington Quay next to Capel Street (then Essex) Bridge, which in those days was the last bridge before the sea. If a new bridge were to be built, it would mean re-locating the Custom House down-river of it. The idea created uproar.

There are five further bridges to the east now, but at that period, tall-masted ships would sail up the Liffey to moor as near as they could get to the old Custom House quayside, there to load

THE CUSTOM HOUSE

❋ The old Custom House on Wellington Quay

or discharge their cargoes. At times, there could be as many as seventy ships lined up along the river, maybe eight abreast, so that one could almost cross the river by hopping from one to another. Cross-river ferries had to weave in and out among them. Ships were becoming bigger and bigger, and a rock known as 'Standfast Dick' near Liffey Street was becoming more difficult to avoid. Even then, some of the larger vessels had to drop anchor farther out in Dublin Bay.

Nonetheless, opposition to re-locating the Custom House down-river was fierce and vitriolic. Powerful commercial interests were involved. All the lucrative businesses connected with shipping and warehousing and trading were concentrated around the existing centre. The idea of moving all this activity to where little existed except fields and swamps seemed insupportable. And of course there were land ownerships and speculative interests on both sides.

However, the Custom House was the headquarters of the Revenue Commissioners and John (later Lord) Beresford, the Chief Revenue Commissioner, was one of the prime movers in favour of re-location. Which brings us to James Gandon.

Gandon was an ex-pupil and friend of William Chambers, an architect who had many Irish connections and who had designed the exquisite Casino at Marino near Dublin for Lord Charlemont. Gandon's friend, Paul Sandby, held a regular Sunday salon, and there Gandon, himself a genial and sociable fellow, met a number of important and influential Irish personalities. On the recommendations of Chambers and Lord Carlow, another of Sandby's circle, Beresford approached young Gandon and asked him to prepare drawings for a new Custom House – this without Gandon even seeing the site. Gandon accepted promptly and set to work straight away. Beresford came to collect the drawings under cover of darkness one wintry night. He wrote:

This business must be kept a profound secret, as long as we can, to prevent clamour, until we have everything secured.

When the powers that be (or were) yielded at last (London was the seat of power at the time), Gandon was more or less smuggled into Ireland to undertake the work, which was 'to commence at once'. Even then he had to be further admonished:

The business is of a delicate nature, and must be managed still with dexterity, having the city [Corporation] of Dublin and a great number of the merchants, together with what is considered as the most desperate of the mob, to contend with.

The opposition was far from resigned to the whole business. In the early stages, Gandon had to stay hidden away, almost a prisoner, relieved only by an invitation to stay at Slane Castle for a while, out of harm's way. He visited the site as rarely as possible, usually in the very early morning. When he did, he carried a cane sword in case he was attacked. When the foundation trenches were opened, the opposition enlisted a mob to fill them in. But it was a fine, warm, sunny day and the mob amused itself by swimming in the trenches instead!

A month after the foundation stone was laid in August 1781, the High Sheriff himself

> . . . *followed by a numerous rabble, with adzes, saws, shovels etc., etc., came in a body on the ground, and levelled that portion of the fence . . . adjoining the North Wall.*

There were many other problems. The swampy site required all of Gandon's ingenuity in laying foundations. A project so big needed a huge team of workmen, and some were brought over from England to supplement the local force. Gandon records that, whereas these were well-behaved and orderly at first, in the end they were more refractory than the locals 'and worse by far as to drunkenness'. There were further attempts at disruption before matters settled down and work was able to proceed.

It is here that the story of the River Gods and of their sculptor, Edward Smyth, begins.

THE RIVER GODS
AND EDWARD SMYTH

The design for the Custom House called for an enormous amount of decorative sculpture. Gandon was unfamiliar with the Irish scene and had been led to believe that the arts were not highly developed in Ireland. Naturally, in the beginning, he relied on those practising sculptors whom he already knew in London, in particular Agostino Carlini and Thomas Bankes, both of whom had worked on Somerset House in London.

However, Gandon also decided to find out for himself whether there were any artists of merit locally. He asked his stone-cutting contractor, Henry Darley, for his advice and Darley immediately recommended one of his employees, Edward Smyth (or Smith, as it is written by Gandon). Gandon gave Smyth some drawings of decorative features and asked him to produce models. Gandon was, he records, 'at once impressed with the masterly, artist-like manner in which they were executed' – so impressed that he decided to offer Smyth the opportunity to submit a design for the Irish Arms, an important feature to surmount one of the pavilions, not telling him that he already had designs in hand from Carlini. The Gandon *Life* tells us that

Smith . . . produced a composition so noble, and so pre-eminently superior, both as to grouping and execution, to that which Carlini had sent, that Mr. Gandon, turning to Darley, said 'This will do;

this is the artist I require; he must go alone, and quit your employment.' He instantly wrote to Mr. Beresford to say that there was no further necessity to send to London for models or sculptures, as he had then found in Dublin an artist capable of the highest works of Art, either as a modeller or sculptor.

✳ Edward Smyth, sculptor of the River Gods

We know little enough of Smyth. He was born in Co. Meath around 1749, son of a 'country stone-cutter'. He came to Dublin when he was still quite young and was apprenticed to Simon Vierpyl, a Flemish sculptor then operating in Dublin. When a competition was opened for a statue of Lord Lucas for the Royal Exchange (now the City Hall), Smyth entered and won. The statue, which can still be seen there in the Round Room, does not have the usual monumental solemnity associated with such subjects. Instead it is intensely naturalistic, full of animation, movement and energy. Its creation was 'a rather astonishing performance', according to C.P. Curran, 'for a young man of very limited opportunity'. This remark echoes Gandon's to the effect that Smyth

> . . . *without having had the advantage of travel, or opportunity of seeing many specimens of sculpture, has given proof of abilities equal to any in the three kingdoms.*

Despite this 'sensational debut', no further commissions seem to have come Smyth's way for the next ten years, during which time he was employed carving ornamental panels and chimney-pieces – which must have been extremely frustrating for an artist of his ability.

Then came his encounter with Gandon. From that point on, he worked on all of Gandon's buildings in

* The statue of Lord Lucas by Edward Smyth stands in the Round Room of the City Hall

Ireland. In addition to the River Gods, Smyth's most noted works include the four Arms of Ireland on the corner pavilions of the Custom House, described by Maurice Craig as 'perhaps the most perfectly architectural sculptures in these islands', and the colossal statue of 'Commerce' which surmounts the dome, as well as other statuary. Smyth was also responsible for the great statue of Moses holding the Tables of Law on the pediment of the Four Courts, as well as the caryatids flanking the entrances of the two wings of the King's Inns.

Smyth died suddenly on 2 August 1812, Gandon eleven years later. In temperament, these two men were complete opposites and one wonders at the terms of their relationship. Gandon was genial, sociable, humorous and outgoing. At the time he came to Gandon's notice, Smyth is described as 'a humble, retiring modest man, subsisting on very slender means in a back room in Mecklenburgh Street'.

* The Arms of Ireland, showing the union of England, Scotland and Ireland. The Shield and Harp are surmounted by the Crown, with the Lion and Unicorn on either side.

THE RIVERS

Symbolic carvings of rivers were familiar in classical Renaissance architecture; they were a feature of Somerset House in London which had been erected a short time before Gandon's Custom House in Dublin took shape. Dublin's riverine sculptures, however, are regarded as 'vastly superior', according to a writer in the *Dublin Evening Post* in September 1787. They form the keystones of the ground-floor arches and represent these Irish rivers.

Boyne
Barrow
Lagan
Liffey
Nore
Shannon
Suir
Bann
Blackwater
Lee
Mourne (i.e. Foyle)
Lough Erne
Slaney

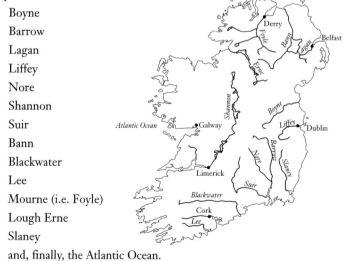

and, finally, the Atlantic Ocean.

The sculptures are laden with the produce of their territories – the cattle, the fruit, the wool, the fish and oysters. Most of them are easily identified by their emblematic embellishments. However, as no formal identifications were recorded at the time, there is some disagreement over a few of them. We give them here as identified by the expert architectural historian, Harold G. Leask, which is how they are generally accepted now.

The heads are carved in Portland stone, each about 90 cm high by more than 30 cm wide (2' 3" x 1'). A set of small wax models of twelve of them is held in the Dublin Civic Museum.

✳ The Liffey Head on O'Connell Bridge

Smyth also carved two riverine heads for Carlisle (now O'Connell) Bridge when it was built in 1790, one representing the Liffey, the other similar to that of the Atlantic Ocean. When the bridge was later rebuilt, the keystones no longer fitted the flattened arches and they were replaced with copies. The two original heads were subsequently mounted on a building (at present occupied by Telecom Éireann) on Sir John Rogerson's Quay, opposite the Custom House and a five-minute walk down-river. From below, this Liffey head looks a bit heavy-jowled, although it might seem more comely when viewed from above or from the side, as it would have been in its original position.

The river heads do not appear to follow any particular plan or logic in their mounting on the Custom House, apart from the placing of the Liffey head in a central position overlooking its river. Their locations are shown in the diagram.

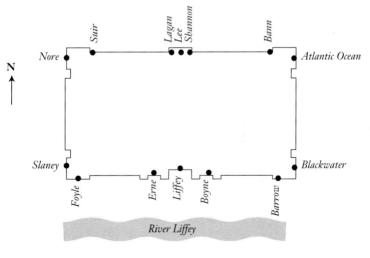

THE LIFFEY

giddy-gaddy, grannyma, gossipaceous Anna Livia. . .[*]

Dublin's river, the Liffey, occupies pride of place overlooking the docks and quayside from the archway over the main river-front entrance of the Custom House. It is the only female head. Why? We do not know. We have no record of the considerations of either sculptor or architect in arriving at the portrayal, which is a great pity. It is true that the Irish *Abha an Life* had become 'Anna Liffey' or even 'Anna Livia' in common parlance. (James Joyce's 'Anna Livia Plurabelle' was more than a century into the future when the Custom House was built.)

Whatever the reasoning, Smyth created her as the idealised classical beauty. He garlanded her with fruit and flowers and crowned her with a trident to indicate her importance as a port.

The Liffey rises in the Wicklow hills, emerging a bare 16 km (10 miles) from Dublin as a thin trickle in the moorland peat bog. If those stone eyes had sight, they might be able to see her own source from her position in the archway. Rather than flowing directly to the sea, however, the Liffey turns her face westward, setting out on a wandering 130-km (80-mile) journey before finally submitting to the sea in Dublin Bay.

The journey takes her through counties Wicklow and Kildare. She helps to fill the great man-made Blessington Lake which

---

*from *Finnegans Wake* by James Joyce

provides both electrical power and drinking water for Dublin city. She braves the 'pooka' of Pollaphuca (the cave of the monster) before flowing westward to the Curragh of Kildare, the *Cuirrech Life* of old from which the river takes her name.

Turning north and eastwards at last, the Liffey meets with its tidal head at Islandbridge on the eastern fringe of the city. Once upon a time, the river spread out from here in a broad muddy terrain before her watery sprawl was tidied and corseted by quays to make the Dublin we know today and to allow the Custom House to be built where it now stands.

THE BOYNE

Moving anti-clockwise (eastwards towards the sea), the Boyne is next encountered. Of all Irish rivers, it is the most legendary and its stories reach back before history began.

The Boyne's head is crowned with ears of wheat and laurel leaves, fitting symbols of the rich lands of Meath through which the river flows. But it is a sad and pensive face, with much to think about: the date emblazoned across its brow, 1690, is the date of the Battle of the Boyne, a tragic or glorious date, according to differing points of view in Irish memory. Here on the banks of the Boyne, James II and William of Orange fought for the throne of England. Though only obliquely an Irish conflict, the defeat of James II marked a turning point in Irish history, the consequences of which are still not fully resolved.

But thousands of years before the Battle of the Boyne, a loop of the river near Slane had a vast significance. At *Brugh na Boinne*, the Palace of the Boyne, stand the most spectacular monuments of European prehistory, the three great passage-graves of Newgrange, Knowth and Dowth, older even than the Great Pyramid of Giza. On the morning of the winter solstice, the rising sun penetrates the long stone-lined passage into the heart of the Newgrange mound and lights up the wall of the deepest recess – a miracle of prehistoric engineering and astronomy. Today, a purpose-built centre explains it all.

There is more. The Boyne flows close to Tara, ancient seat of the High Kings, and through the hunting-ground of the legendary hero Cúchulainn. He it was who single-handedly defended Ulster from the armies of Queen Maeve of Connacht in the epic *Táin Bó Cuailnge*, the Cattle Raid of Cooley, a battle fought over a champion bull.

The Boyne rises almost due west of Dublin in the region of Edenderry and then sweeps in an upward curve to Drogheda. Dubliners can be surprised to find themselves crossing the Boyne on the road to Galway.

THE BARROW

This is one of the heads about which there is some disagreement. Is it the Barrow? Or the Nore? In fact, they are sister rivers, similar in aspect and both flowing southwards to converge above New Ross in Co. Waterford, continuing on as one river to the sea and picking up a third, the Suir, along the way.

The architectural historian, Harold Leask, inclines towards identifying this one as the Barrow and we will be guided by him.

What a gloomy face it is, with its great down-turned mouth, almost comical in its sullenness. And whether Barrow or Nore, there is little to be gloomy about. Both rivers flow through rich and pleasant pastoral lands. Both are famous for fish. The gloomy mouth does indeed spill out a rich cascade of fish and water-weed, forming a kind of beard. The other strong feature is a sheep sprawled over the top of the head, its forelegs framing the forehead. Maybe it was once sheep-country, but we have no references to this effect. Two vases pour water down the sides of the face, which may be an acknowledgment of the sistership of the two rivers.

The Barrow rises on the northern slopes of the Slieve Bloom mountains north of Mountrath and flows eastwards at first before taking up its southward course near Monasterevan. It is a most tranquil and picturesque cruising river, sought out by people looking for a change from the wide waters of the Shannon. It flows past quiet villages, old monastic settlements and fine estates, under graceful stone bridges. Carlow Castle is an imposing ruin overlooking the river. At Leighlinbridge there is a great gathering of waters. The village of St Mullins is named for St Moling who founded a great monastic centre in this beautiful location in the seventh century, parts of which still survive. Just below it, the Barrow is joined by the Nore, and the combined rivers collect the Suir before 'the Three Sisters' meet the sea.

THE BLACKWATER

The next keystone is not, as one might expect, the Nore. Instead we must move south-west to the fringes of Waterford and into Co. Cork.

The Munster Blackwater (known as such to distinguish it from a lesser Blackwater up-country) is indeed a saturnine head but, appropriately, a cascade of fishes flows over its forehead, for the Blackwater was, and is, one of Ireland's great angling rivers. Crowning the head above the multitude of fishes is a basket piled high with apples. The fertile valley of the Blackwater was famous for its orchards in the eighteenth century. The *History of Waterford* (Smith, 1746) says:

> *In the west of this county ... our cyder has of late years been brought to great perfection; and besides enough for our own consumption, some hundreds hogsheads are yearly, in good fruit seasons, sent by sea to Dublin and other places.*

Like the other rivers of the south-west, the Blackwater follows the west/east valleys between the sandstone hills before making a sharp turn southwards at Lismore to enter the sea at Youghal Bay.

With steep wooded banks along much of its course, the Blackwater is regarded as one of the most beautiful of the rivers. Its route is full of interest all the way from its source near the Kerry border. Mallow boasts a small private vineyard and Mallow Castle has a herd of white fallow deer, descendants of a pair which were a gift from Queen Elizabeth I. Lismore, though only a tiny town, is an unforgettable place. The Duke of Devonshire's castle overlooking the river is the most spectacularly romantic of all Ireland's castles and its atmosphere permeates the surrounding town and countryside. Youghal, where the Blackwater spills itself into the sea, is an old walled seaport town. Its main street is spanned by a clock tower which was once a gate in the town walls, then a prison and now, more happily, a museum.

THE ATLANTIC OCEAN

The Atlantic is next in the sequence, near the north-east corner of the building. It declares its name in writing – and it is as well, considering that it faces east, towards the Irish Sea, with its back to the west and the far-off Atlantic seaboard.

It is a fine, boldly modelled face. Dolphins play among the weed-like curls of the beard. The head bears a diadem of pearls and above it, in the centre, is a trident surmounted by a crescent moon, symbolising the ebb and flow of the tides. There are navigational aids too, a binnacle on one side bearing the word 'Atlantic', a compass on the other.

Why the choice of 'the rough and rude Atlantic, the thunderous, the wide' for representation, rather than the Irish Sea over which most of Dublin's trade might be expected to travel and to which the Custom House was adjacent? Probably no better reason than its size and importance. Admittedly there was a long-established trade between Spain and Ireland's west coast, mainly in wines, but this would not equal the day-to-day traffic across the Channel on the east. Neither Gandon nor Smyth could have foreseen that half a century after their work was completed, the Atlantic would assume an enormous importance for a population in the grip of famine. Thousands of the starving poor took ship from Galway and other western ports, hoping for a new and better life in the New World. Some crossed the Irish Sea rather than the

Atlantic; they are commemorated in a sculpture on the quayside close to the Custom House – a pitiful procession of figures clutching their bundles, on their way to they knew not what.

Ireland can thank the North Atlantic Drift – the Gulf Stream – for keeping it, in winter, the warmest place in the world at the same latitude.

THE BANN

Northwards now. The Bann is the most jovial of all the faces. Could it be that the presence of breweries along its course explains this cheerfulness? The berries clustering around the brows are probably hops. The head is swathed in turban-like folds of linen, topped with what looks like flax: the Bann country was famous for its flax-growing and linen weaving. Strings of pearls criss-cross the turban, a reminder that this was once one of a number of rivers noted for fresh-water pearls.

The Bann is an important northern river. It rises high in the Mourne mountains just east of Newry, very close to the sea and Carlingford Lough. Instead of taking what looks like an obvious course, however, it flows north-westwards instead and its journey to the sea takes almost 130 km (80 miles) rather than just about five. But what a journey! Half-way along its course, it widens out to create the enormous shallow Lough Neagh, by far the largest lake in Ireland or Great Britain. From its north-eastern corner, the Upper Bann continues northwards, draining the lake into the North Atlantic close to the town of Coleraine, its entry overlooked by the exquisite cliff-top Mussenden Temple of Downhill.

Lough Neagh is famous for its eel-fishing, so it is surprising that this is not indicated. (Perhaps the product of the hops made the sculptor forget!)

The poet Seamus Heaney, who grew up nearby, has a long verse-sequence on the lake:

At Toomebridge where it sluices towards the sea
They've set new gates and tanks against the flow.
From time to time they break the eels' journey
And lift five hundred stone in one go.

Ireland's most perfect Round Tower stands in the town of Antrim, on Lough Neagh's north-eastern corner.

THE SHANNON

This is a calm face, youthful when compared to several others. Oak leaves and acorns are piled around the head, which is crowned with a trident. Cornucopias spill a wealth of fruit and grain over the forehead and down the cheeks.

Spenser wrote of 'the spacious Shannon, spreading like a sea'. The old legends tell how the maiden Sinann of the Tuatha De Danann, an ancient magical tribe, came to the Shannon Pot, the river's source, to find the secrets of wisdom which lay there. But the well rose up and drowned her and ever since the river bears her name.

This is Ireland's most noble river. The Shannon Pot is in the foothills of the Cuilcagh mountains, north of Dowra in Co. Cavan. It is a steep-sided pool, deep and dark, and hung all around with willows, and a few hazel trees, always known for their magic. From its source, it flows slowly and majestically for 270 km (170 miles) through the midland plains, almost dividing Ireland down the centre. Only when nearing Limerick does it hurry its pace for a short distance, in an onrush which nowadays feeds a hydro-electric generating station. From Limerick, its gradually widening estuary stretches a further 100 km (65 stately miles) to the Atlantic.

Along its way, the river spreads into beautiful lakes and complex backwaters. Lough Ree and Lough Derg are the largest, but many regard Lough Key as the most beautiful, nestling as it does among wooded hills. Old castles and monastic settlements dot the shores and islands, as the great river was the main highway through the heart of Ireland in medieval times and before. French wine travelled up the Shannon to the monastic city of Clonmacnois, now slumbering serenely on the river shore just south of Athlone.

The Shannon was always a cruising paradise. In 1995, it was joined with the Erne (q.v.) by a canal to provide more than 800 km (500 miles) of untroubled leisure waterways, unequalled anywhere in Europe.

The Lee

The Lee is the river of Cork, Ireland's southern capital, and exiled Corkmen and women sing of it nostalgically at any given opportunity:

Where I sported and played, 'neath each green leafy shade,
On the banks of my own lovely Lee.

Here we see it with a noble and vigorous face, with hair like ocean waves. The head is surmounted by an upturned anchor from which a cable stretches to each side over ships laden with barrels and bales. Cork has always been known as a merchant city, and its immense harbour has served its long mercantile tradition. Spenser wrote of

The spreading Lee, that like an island fayre
Encloseth Corke with his divided flood.

That is because the river flows through Cork in two separate channels, giving rise to the need for the numerous bridges which are a feature of the city, as are its hilly streets. And regularly, the chimes of 'the Bells of Shandon' float down from their hilltop spire to drift along the river banks.

The Lee's allegorical head looks north from the Custom House rather than south as one would expect, but its importance is probably indicated by its central position, directly opposite that of the Liffey on the south front.

The source of the Lee is a deep and lovely lake called Gougane Barra (Barra's rocky cave), close to the borders of Co. Kerry. Wooded mountains rise steeply all around it and streams gush down the slopes. It is named for Saint Finbarr, or Finn (the fair-headed) Barra, patron and founder of Cork city, who had his hermitage there. Over a thousand years later, pilgrims still gather at the lake to honour the saint on 25 September each year.

THE LAGAN

The Lagan presents a serene, lightly-bearded face, draped around the chin and neck with folds of cloth, presumably linen. Two swans with entwined necks crown the head, on a nest of bulrushes and flowers.

Belfast, capital of Northern Ireland, is where the Lagan meets the sea, flowing through beautiful Belfast Lough to the bleak North Channel between Ireland and Scotland. The Children of Lir, turned into swans, spent three hundred unhappy years in this cold and turbulent sea, as told in one of Ireland's ancient tales.

Belfast linen is still a family heirloom in many households. The blue flax fields of the Lagan Valley were famous in days gone by. The arrival of synthetic fabrics put an end to the industry but, ironically, linen has now made a comeback in popularity. The fields of blue flax were beautiful to look at but the harvesting and treatment of the crop was hard and unpleasant work. The flax was 'retted' (in fact, allowed to rot) in ponds, then spread to dry before the fibre was extracted. The smell from this process was as nasty as the growing plant was sweet. Later, the woven lengths of cloth were spread to bleach across the fields, growing white against the green meadows, by all accounts a wondrous sight.

Ship-building was Belfast's other great industry. It was out of the shipyards of the Lagan that the *Titanic* slid at birth, the 'unsinkable' ship which met its watery death on its maiden voyage in April 1912 with the loss of 1,513 lives.

Along its way, the Lagan flows through Lisburn town and curves around near Lurgan to pass through the country where a schoolmaster called Patrick Prunty, or Brunty, or Brontë (the name has several variations), lived before going to England and fathering that extraordinary family of writers.

The industrial bustle of Belfast is in strong contrast to the quiet of the knobbly hills above Ballynahinch where the river is born, close to where an ancient dolmen has stood, little changed, for some thousands of years.

THE SUIR

. . . Where the thrush and the robin their sweet notes entwine
On the banks of the Suir that flows down by Mooncoin.

The Suir joins the lower reaches of the Nore and Barrow (qq. v.) at Waterford city, becoming the third river of those which have come to be known as 'the Three Sisters'.

Its source lies a short distance south of that of the Nore near the mountain known as the Devil's Bit, inside the triangle of Nenagh, Roscrea and Templemore. Whereas the Nore wanders off north-eastwards for a while, the Suir takes a more direct route southwards. Shortly after flowing through the town of Thurles, it laps at the feet of Holy Cross Abbey. There are few more picturesque abbeys than this. It was founded by the Cistercians in the twelfth century and has been so beautifully restored that one can almost hear in the imagination the plain chant of the monks echoing over the waters.

The Suir by-passes the Rock of Cashel but swirls against the massive walls of Cahir Castle with its towers and battlements. It turns eastwards shortly after, via Clonmel (the meadow of honey) and Carrick-on-Suir with its Elizabethan mansion of Black Tom, 10th Earl of Ormond, and on under the shelter of Slievenamon, the mountain of women, to join its sister rivers at Waterford harbour. The Mooncoin of the song is on the lovely road between

Carrick-on-Suir and the city.

The Suir creates a straight quarter-mile-long quay through Waterford city. Like a number of other port towns, Waterford was founded by the Vikings and the tower built in 1003 AD by Reginald the Norseman still stands intact by the quayside.

Henry II sailed up the Suir in 1171 to claim the city – and Ireland – for the crown. At a later stage in a stormy history, Richard II sailed in with a large army to wrestle with local reassertions of Gaelic authority.

THE NORE

ister-river to the Barrow and Suir, as depicted in stone the Nore is sombre and sleepy. A seine-net, complete with ropes and floats, is draped around the head, and fish escape from it down the cheeks. There is some argument about this identification, particularly in relation to the Barrow (q.v.), and it could be said to have been arrived at by a process of elimination. The Nore was only one of several rivers noted for net-fishing.

Like the Suir, the Nore rises close to the Devil's Bit mountain near Roscrea and wanders north-eastwards towards Mountrath before turning southwards and flowing more or less parallel to the Barrow as far as New Ross in Co. Waterford, where it unites with it before the combined rivers are joined by the Suir.

Today the Nore is noted as the river of Kilkenny city, an important place since very early times and which was from time to time the seat of parliament. Kilkenny still retains many of its medieval features, with winding streets and narrow laneways. St Canice's Cathedral stands much as it did in the fifteenth century, and a Round Tower, much older, stands close by. There are old abbeys, churches and colleges, but most dramatic of all is Kilkenny Castle, standing on the banks of the river. The massive fortification, once the home of the Earls and Dukes of Ormonde, now belongs to the people of Kilkenny and much of the city's social life revolves around it and its gardens and parkland. (The castle's stables were so advanced for their time that someone remarked that they must have been designed by a horse.) Lovely tree-lined walks spread along the river banks and game fish still thrive in its waters.

At Abbeyleix, the river flows through the parklands of Abbey Leix demesne, former home of the Viscounts de Vesci. The demesne woodlands are famous for their bluebell season. Jerpoint Abbey is close to the Nore near Thomastown on a small tributary called the Eoir. Though in a ruined state, it is a lovely, serene place with its cloisters and intriguing stone carvings.

THE SLANEY

Crabs, scallops, oysters, ears of corn – these are the embellishments of the head which has been identified as the Slaney. 'For ale and oysters Wexford is noted as having the best on earth' is quoted by Hore in his *History of Wexford*. Even today, a large share of Ireland's mussels are cultivated in Wexford harbour.

The Slaney rises in the Wicklow mountains, under the north-west shoulder of Lugnaquilla. It flows south through Baltinglass with its still-graceful ruined abbey, through Bunclody and Enniscorthy, thence to Wexford and its wide harbour, pouring itself forcefully through a narrow gorge at Ferrycarrig (just north of Wexford town) where a castle stands on one outcrop and a round tower-style monument on the other, like guardian portals. Its course lies roughly parallel to those of the Barrow and Nore.

Wexford, much of which is built along the river front, is an attractive old walled town with narrow, winding streets. Its embattled memories include the stay of Henry II in Selskar Abbey in 1172, doing penance for the murder of St Thomas à Becket. Many of the dramatic and bitter events of the 1798 Rising took place on the banks of the Slaney.

Apart from the cultivation of shellfish, today's main preoccupation for the people of Wexford is their famous Festival Opera held every year in October. Then, some of the world's finest artists come to perform in the town's tiny theatre, an achievement which represents the victory of mind over matter, as the main resource on which it is founded is the willing and voluntary dedication of the citizenry.

Birds love this river. The mouth of the Slaney is a famous nature reserve where half the whole world population of Greenland White-fronted Geese spends the winter.

THE FOYLE

The grim, forbidding face of the Foyle allows for no
argument about its identity. Across its brow, over a
victorious wreath of laurel, is emblazoned the date 1689.
Above it, the prow of a ship breaks through a great cable slung
between two castles.

Derry (or Londonderry as many know it – the 'London' was
added in 1613 by charter of James I) straddles the Foyle just
before it becomes Lough Foyle, a huge span of water opening to
the North Sea. The date on the stone brow commemorates the
most notable incident in the history of Derry, one still celebrated
by a portion of Derry's citizens.

The Siege of Derry of 1689 arose out of the battle of the kings
for the British throne: most of Ireland rallied to the rightful James
II, but Derry decided for William of Orange. They closed the city
gates against the loyalist troops and a cannon was fired against
King James himself outside the gates. The king's army threw a
boom across the Foyle, at the spot where Boom Hall now stands,
to halt any aid to the garrison. The siege lasted almost eight
months, until relieving ships at last breached the boom, bringing
supplies to the city and defeat to James.

The Foyle is a gathering of several rivers from widely differing
watersheds which come together at or above the twin towns of
Lifford and Strabane, which stand on either bank. They include
the Finn from Donegal (from Fintown), the Owenkillew and the

Glenally from the Sperrin mountains, and the Mourne which flows down from Tyrone. There is even one called the Fairy Water! Their combined lengths dwarf the Foyle's own, which is all of just 32 km (20 miles), though Lough Foyle is as long again as the river and almost as wide at its southern reaches.

THE ERNE

Here is a head which might well be submerged in the river, so wavy with water-weed and flowing with fishy life is it. There is a salmon; there is a pike with an eel issuing from its jaws; there are shellfish and small fish of all sorts. And this is a river which deserves them all.

The Erne is the most complex of all the Irish rivers. From its source in Co. Cavan near Ballyjamesduff, it winds an incredibly serpentine way northwards, forming countless lakelets, islands and backwaters. At Enniskillen, it widens into Lower Lough Erne where its complexity diminishes.

This astonishing waterway makes a cruising paradise and has in recent times been joined by a canal to the Shannon system, the two combined creating the most wonderful cruising ground in western Europe. A lifetime could be spent exploring the intricacies of shore, islands and inlets of the Erne.

Castle Coole, on the shores of Upper Lough Erne, is one of Ireland's finest classical mansions. Devinish Island near Enniskillen has the peaceful remains of a medieval monastery and Round Tower. Some miles to the north, White Island bears fantastical sculptures of an unknown origin. And where the road crosses the lake at Dreenan, two still more ancient effigies look balefully at the passing scene, which they are thought to have done for nigh on two thousand years.

The fish life indicated in the stone head still brings anglers congregating to the Erne's shores. In the region of its upper waters, the complexity of tiny lakes and little drumlin mounds give the impression that every house and farm has its own private and secluded fishing lake and hill.

It reaches the sea at Ballyshannon. The poet William Allingham bid 'Adieu to Ballyshanny and the Winding Banks of Erne' in one of his best-known poems.

REFERENCES

Curran, C.P., 'Mr. Edward Smyth, Sculptor', *Architectural Review*, February 1947.

Gandon James (jnr) and T.J. Mulvany, *The Life of James Gandon Esq.*, Dublin 1846.

Leask, Harold G., 'Dublin's Custom House: the Riverine Sculptures', *Journal of the Royal Society of Antiquaries of Ireland*, 1945.

McParland, Edward, *James Gandon: Vitruvius Hibernicus*, London 1985.

Office of Public Works, *The Custom House Dublin*.

THE WOLFHOUND GUIDE TO
DUBLIN MONUMENTS
Elizabeth Healy

Packed with information on dozens of monuments, many of which have become so familiar to Dubliners that we have stopped noticing them. This book looks at how the monuments, memorials, statues, public sculptures and corporate art of Dublin reflect the history of the city and that of the nation.

ISBN 0 86327 637 7

THE WOLFHOUND GUIDE TO
THE IRISH HARP EMBLEM
Séamas Ó Brógáin

This is the story of one of the oldest and most distinctive national emblems in the world. From the obscurity of the thirteenth century to the present day, its history has often been concealed in myth. Now the familiar badge of the Irish State, the harp has been our most characteristic musical instrument since the eleventh century.

ISBN 0 86327 635 0

THE WOLFHOUND GUIDE TO
THE IRISH WOLFHOUND
Muriel Monsell Bremner

A treasure trove of everything you ever wanted to know about this great dog's close identity with Ireland's history, plus lots of interesting things you never thought to ask. Renowned for their strength, famed for their courage and cherished for their sensitivity and loyalty, these dogs have been immortalised in legend and song.

ISBN 0 86327 636 9